The
POEMS
of
LOVE

♥

Aleksandra Malchrzyk

Bitsy Tales 2024

to all those lovers
whom I did not have

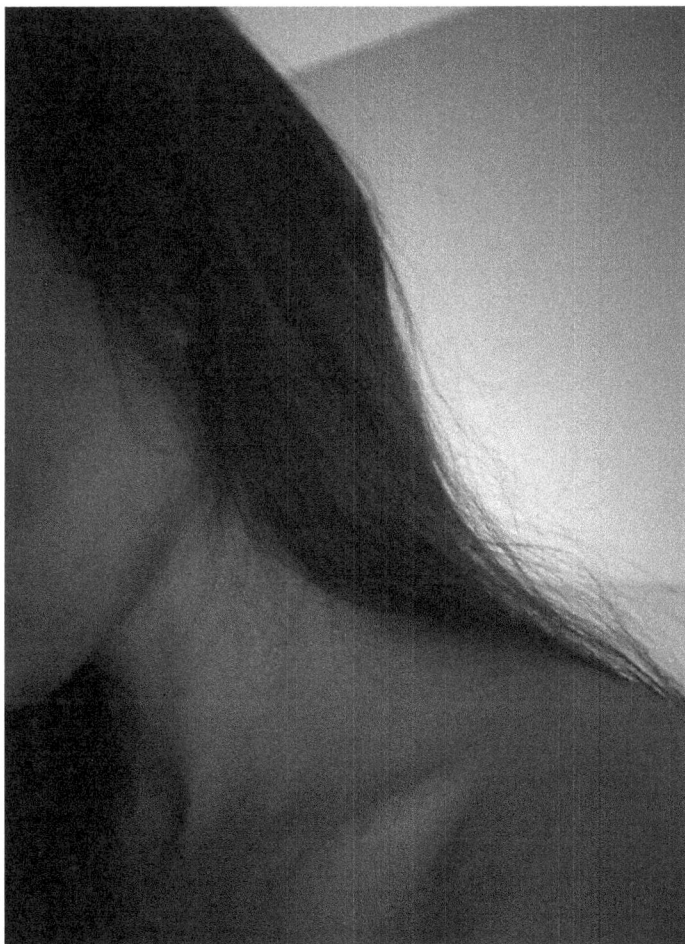

shhh, take my hand and let me take you on a journey through the words, let me show you worlds created that are filled with night and dusk, let yourself be charmed and sated by the magic of the verse, let me bind you with those fetters that are spells in poems cursed

A.

silk she wore

And the silk she wore fell to the floor.

And what was underneath was his, his, his.

The air was heavy, hardened with heaves, the night's darkest plumage enwrapped them with ease.

The whispers, the sighs, the smallest delights were in exchange, abundant, like rage.

She died a little, shaped like an arch, forbidden fruit — to leave her so parched.

the search for gold

his lips, impatient, searched for the gold

and searched-for she was, wanted, not
long

her body of burnished gold colour
sealed

awaiting the key her master would wield

the silence reigned but it was broke

by sound of the key finding the lock

the gold was his, and no longer hers

flood of satiation caught both unawares

the Schiele red

to him she was Schiele and red was her crown

the curves, the shadows, the eyes, and the mouth

drowned in the light that was no longer present

oblivious, murky, and dry as the desert

///

to him she was Schiele, defiant and daring

the body, the hips, the pose, and the bearing

hidden in shades, in hues that were absent

silent, untold, and heady as absinthe

wild cherry trees

among the wild cherry trees she trod
softly

he followed gently, like dog loved most
coyly

the branches her obscured so neatly

the fruit screened steps she took so
measly

///

in orchard thus they wandered meekly

the sap grew denser, the light got prickly

two figures lost in hot pursuit

lustily looking for sweetness of fruit

apostrophe

feed me atropine for I am hungry for
love that's poison

turn me into heresiarch, no more saintly
hymn singing

transform me into a zealot with your
mesmerist's eyes

mould me into a shape that fits your fist
followingly

///

stamp me with a mark that bears your
name on it

transmute me into air which feeds your
lungs each day

see me changed into what your dreams
are made of

watch me become your blood and your
veins

darkly, darkly

darkly, darkly, come toward me

make me helpless, lusty, reckless

make me burn with hellish fire

come toward me, I require

///

say my name as spell so binding

follow me, and follow blindly

turn me into your own always

have me as your precious goddess

///

slowly, slowly, move toward me

make me careless, bold, and hungry

make me want for fruit forbidden

come toward me, I so bid you

///

spell my name and say it loudly

want me now, and want me madly

turn me into your own deity

give new name to omneity

…

darkly, darkly,

oh do come toward me

make haste

Make haste!

spend your days with me, and nights, too

stick to me like hardest glue

snatch me from the sight of others

want me so, don't want another

///

turn me into your own goddess

worship me, forget all others

make me yours until forever

fight the urge this tie to sever

you fed me roses

you fed me roses and I concurred — the
hunger appeased, the flowers all gone

veins turned red ruby, eyes bloodshot
like fire

capitulate I, and I so desire — the words
that are crimson, the sky that is lead

no one predicted and no one cared. The
war that's ongoing, the cards are all laid

so brutal, so shrill, so no prisoners

///

you fed me violets and they tasted of
rain. The hue, the flavour, the soil that's
deep red

flowers all gone, the colours remain —
deep purple, deep sorrow, deep all
colours wept

stars in her soul

stars collapsed and one by one fell
down the sky and entered her soul

with eyes fixated and hands aflame he
searched her soul for stars ablaze

and when he found them they turned so
prickly

he could not touch them, they shone
magically

he tried to rip them out with force, but
they defended themselves perforce

and so they stayed where they were,
enlightened darkness with warmth and
glare

and thus he stayed by her side, too to
tend to light with zealot's ardour

sin

practise sin like others do gods

make orisons turn to dust

call my name *de profundis*

eulogise what not there is

///

exegeses scribe profoundly

homilies omit entirely

say your vespers without meaning

then blaspheme with pious feeling

her centre

with his lips travelling toward her centre

she threw back her head and waited,
waited

with eyes closed shut but lips a bit open

with little groans the silence was broken

///

with much devotion he proceeded

with moans the groans were
superseded

she gushed toward him with bated
breath

his journey ended in landscape wet

see me walk into a room

see me walk into a room, slowly, naked

brave the gloom

follow me with eyes that burn, closely, keenly

every turn

make me come in your direction, quietly,

but full of tension

welcome me with arms wide open

seal me in them thus unbroken

ocean of lust

here I am and there you are and in
between an ocean of lust

a river flows to and fro, carrying the
message that all is not lost

the depths so hidden, the whirls so
braved, another day awaits with much
haste

to me hurry still, to me hurry so, brave
the dark ocean, arrive on my shore!

lost in lust

lost in lust and nearly drowned

whirring, whirling, losing ground

lost in thoughts and nearly there

praying, pleading, pleased to dare

///

lost in life and hardly found

seeking, stirring, stomping ground

lost in time and spent in vain

wailing, wanting, wildest reign

Bursa figs

figs, my favourite

you fed me

and with them

the bitterness of breaks

in between

wild wonder

her eyes glittered wildly, like those of a tigress

as she beheld his future prowess

her body shook, like that of a leaf

as she imagined his thrusts so deep

///

his eyes beheld her in fullness of glory

as she allowed him to read her like story

his body heaved, like that of a panther

as he accomplished the hunt for wild wonder

the pearls, the truffles, the silk, the wine

the finer things in life

the pearls, the truffles, the silk, the wine

I want to with you experience each day

to get satiated by gifts of your hands

///

the noble feelings that soul elate

the awe, the love, the lustful wait

I want to with you feel each day

to get fulfilled in every way

///

the little pleasures that please one so

the kiss, the touch, the moments ago

I want to with you share to the brim

to have a life that's more than a dream

those nights, those nights

those nights, those nights

full of fulfilment

the sky was a-blushing

the stars fled the firmament

///

your body on mine and then right behind

your body on mine and wild was the
night

the silence that reigned once moans
turned to quiet

the shadows asleep, the bodies ceased
riot

you were the sand

when the storm hit the shore and I was
water

you were the sand I chose to slaughter

with throttling wetness, with lashes of
fury

I tried you under me ruthlessly bury

///

so under my waves you were buried

with passion, without the onus of hurry

each grain was captured by tiny droplet

the wetness beheld your countenance
conquered

from thigh to hip

from thigh to hip, from lips to neck

from foot to knee, from back to front

from gasp to moan, from cold to hot

the adventure in bodies has just begun

opening lines

those opening lines to you were
dedicated

and the drama that followed to you was
subjected

happy and hollow, hollow and happy

your edges blurry, my vision myopic

how have you managed my king
become

when I thought of kingdoms I had need
none

how have you shown yourself to be

the man by whose side I yearn to be

star tracing

he traced the stars reflected in her body
with his finger

slowly, from point to point, from star to
star

there were more stars on her thighs
than anywhere else and so he traced,
traced, and traced

some of the stars shot and fell, some of
them stayed where they were

the longer he traced, the fewer the stars
became

when none was left another galaxy
called his name

hear bones curl

shake your head in disbelief, throw
away the mind that's weak

bend so backwards that it hurts, bend
again and hear bones curl

sin and pray with utmost pleasure, have
hopes dashed by empty treasure

beg your way through lifeless deserts,
have your share of guilty pleasures

I am a well

I am a well, deep, dark, and narrow

and to your mouth I surge and I wallow

sweetest of waters I have to offer

thirstiest of thirsts to quench I proffer

///

come drink from depths to you unknown

have just a sip, then have some more

forget yourself, abandon shame

come drink at well that waits so tame

of poetry say no more

whisper to me filthiest words

of poetry say no more

make my shame just disappear

make your wishes to me clear

///

stand aside and watch me roar

come then closer, like you swore

when so close don't spare me any

kisses, lashes, one of many

say vespers to me

If you don't believe in magic, yield to
mine.

If you don't believe in god, make me
your own.

If you don't like pears, taste mine.

If you don't pray, say vespers to me.

If you don't know, make believe.

If you don't yield, yield to me.

dark-plumed

replete with the colours of a morning sky

primaeval, dark-plumed like a bird that
soars high

kept like a legend in their dry souls

barely awaken to world that's so small

///

frugal and fitful, fancy and faithful

tones hued by passion, moribund,
shaken

keep me like fire, uphold like a value

let me not perish unless you desire

contrition

prayerfully, he she explored

with avid fingers, mouth, and a tongue

there was no need to ask permission

for she to him yielded like sin to
contrition

wild, wild, wild

with your whispers so mild you made
me wild, wild, wild

with your biting so hard you made me
scarred, scarred, scarred

with your ruthless pursuit you made me
mute, mute, mute

with your devoted self you made me
yearn, yearn, yearn

cover me in smaragds, cover me in rubies

cover me in smaragds, cover me in
rubies

with a madman's passions, give yourself
to these

thoughts, feelings, wants, and needs
that you harbour

though they be what makes your fears
grander

though they may be threatening heaven,
though they may seem like dreams that
come never

ignore the urge to seem in control,
ignore the need to conquer the soul

but do approach and progress slowly
toward the peaks that rule so snowy

for I am queen of summits frustrating

for I am queen for king much a-waiting

when on velvet you had me

when on velvet you had me

it was dawn that was breaking

and my heart was a-flutter, and my legs
were a-shaking

the stars above, the moon in full
lightness

the cries for more defied the world's
laughter

and I knew you gave me whatever you
had

the depth of your being, the wants of
your life

those I received with faith and with love

for your life is mine, and mine is yours

but your eyes speak

lips sealed with invisible wax

but your eyes speak

and volumes they have written with
words that are hidden

in between lines creeps meaning, in
between lines you tread and I follow

I like to read… the poetry of your eyes,
your gestures speak to my mind, and
even deeper

the words come except they don't

the light has shone but now it won't

the pyres are burning, made not to
measure, the smoke has risen, cruelly,
brazen

why don't you say what your eyes can't
speak?

why don't you turn away from the meek?

take courage, my love, be bold, I thus
beg you

become of steel that troubles won't bend
you

say what you will and into my ear

it will be received without any fear

canto after canto

canto after canto I call your name

but the deepest oblivion renders you deaf

time after time I beckon in vain

but the smallest gestures drown in darkest pain

line after line I write to you

but the messenger is shot in furious gloom

verse after verse to you I write

but the page and the ink are equally white

hussars, bullets, cannons, sabres

hussars may drag me away from you

but have no power to rob me of you

bullets may turn me into a sieve

but won't make me lose in love belief

cannons may turn me into a mush

but will not take heart with love a-flush

sabres may cut me to the bone

but will not touch marrow you have
become

epinicion

into my ear sing your epinicion

I want to hear its every word

you fought bravely with lots of gumption

on every front beneath the moon

///

the laurel rests on heavy brow

the medals chest embellish

and there I rest in front of you

the prize you shall now relish

the smallest poem

the smallest poem for you I would write

to thus express the passion of might

of brightest hue it blazes wildly

of grandest trees it swallows fruit aptly

///

it burns and it swallows what there might
be

it wants to prove the visions of seers

but you know better, with heart so still

that I do love you with strongest of wills

wine-stained lips

wine-stained lips, deep blue and
deepening

blurry eyes yet pleasure seeking

your lips try hard to kiss off the blue

your eyes in mine drown in its hue

///

let me get you drunk with just my
presence

my body, my moans, my satiation never

be carried away by bottomless lust

drink wine from my lips

with grandest of thirsts

water reflected in her naked body

water reflected in her naked body

resting by wetness, solemnly silent

his just right next to and equally tired

of lake lustre, shadows, of waves that
came by her

///

water and wetness — her two elements

when so combined, gone is the shy

her hunger sated with breaths unabated

with lake the witness and she the
mistress

sweetest of treats

with her hands behind her back

she could feel him in and out

buried face in crispy bed sheet

on the way to sweetest of treats

the tenth

against the tenth I wish to sin

for you are worth of every thing

against the law I want to march

for you are why my mind is parched

against the custom I yearn to go

for you are path and I'm its stones

against the world I wish to rise

for you are to become just mine

the mango grove

in the mango grove you tasted my fruit

yellowy flesh, wet, ripe, and smooth

nightingales sang with all their might

yet drowned they were by groans of delight

you came away fed and so pleased

for you have feasted on best that there is

then you came back to have some more

you could not forget the treasures grove holds

rob my orchard

rob my orchard, full of fruit

apples, pears, and peaches too

steal the key that fits my lock

here awaits the wettest loch

///

open doors and let it flow

taste it much and taste it so

so that you will not forget

how it heaved and how it begged

///

rob me often, rob me much

find the pleasure like no such

send me into awful frenzy

make me object of much envy

///

place your honour on the rocks

drink it up and ask for more

tell the tale and make it climax

read the play with all its mad acts

///

fruit for picking, sweet and ripe

search for lips, hope yours to find

so that juice can find its way

into abyss grey yet gay

///

mould me into shapes of old

hold me, hold me, hold some more

of your dreams I wish to be

keep me like a sacred thing

I am patience and you are lead

Am I the woman you love?

I demand to know.

///

I'd like to be, if truth be told

for fate us threw together so

it seems unfair to have to wait

but I am patience and you are lead

the ways are twisted and roads
unmapped

with lowered eyes, I bide my time

minute by minute, I pine for thee

seeking to beat eternity

a foreign shore

you are a foreign shore I wish to explore

you are a wooden church I want to burn

you are a pear whose shape I trace

with fingers, with eyes, with little grace

you are a lover I wish to take

you are a sinner I beg to forget

you are a god I wish to worship

with fervent prayers and guilty
conscience

dark woods

dark woods but then light as a feather

you and I, ensconced, safely together

my rhymes are simple and unrefined

the blood that flows is red but not wine

///

I wish to snatch you and make you mine

the gems, the diamonds, the jewels I
find

in depths in you hidden, in halls that are
new

with every hit I strike gold that is you

fruit of delight

flowers grew out of her mouth

for she was fertile inside and out

the seed he sought to sow abundant

her lands unraided, her will redundant

///

the raid took place and seed took root

the body flowered in spasms and shoots

after a time a tree sprung out

with branches of fire and fruit of delight

of pleasure lessons

the air was saturated with evening
vapours

she on mist reclined, awake yet delirious

when mist was trodden by heavy
presence

she only discovered when his hands
embraced her

///

presence grew heavy, presence grew
hard

her will gave way to steps that trod fast

in mist enshrouded, oblivious, hidden

of pleasure lessons she learnt unbridled

like dust

I broke into fire under your hands

somehow you managed to stay in
charge

from red to black and then into ash

the two of us wind swept like dust

fire, brimstone

"On your knees!" I said and said it rightly

"Worship me, worship, like the queen
almighty!"

"I will you worship for I am slave

to your love like a queenly knave."

So I said: "Serve me well,

for my demands are those of hell:

fire, brimstone, lots of heat

all-consuming, bold and sweet!"

meeting at dawn

I sent you a letter but it came too late

the edges frayed, the contents stale

I tried to call but you were not home

the lights were out, the walls were gone

I begged to charm you with words of lust

but you were made of resistance,
heavier than rust

I tried and tried, my will went awry

and yours went too and met mine at
dawn

stain me

stain me with yourself

like wine does sheet when no one's to
blame

your wine full-bodied, potent, and dry

each taste I get makes me want to go
back

and come again until there's no more

emptiness rules in glass that was full

but you know how much I love your wine

and to my tastes caters your cellar each
night

cerulean of ocean's hounds

wrapped in blue like heaven bound

cerulean of ocean's hounds

afloat, airborne, celestial dome

her body shaped like moon a-glow

bellow

my long wait still longer

the sky turns grey

bellow, bellow, the wind of change

Astarte

Astarte has me in her power

the rage I feel, that me devours

I seek to quell, to drown in Styx

and fill the void with love unique

oceans drained

my oceans drained but secretly for you
flow

for you like to swim in waters without
shores

when through my waves I feel you sail

my wetness grows, your might I hail

we revolve around each other

we revolve around each other

closer, harder, not together

space that's filled with doubt and
shyness

breached by burning deeply glances

reive my lands

reive my lands, take them from me

plunder, rob, and let me not be

for into one two are melded

into sameness by fate belted

futile supplication

my God, you won't help me however
much I pray

for you have gone to pastures new and
found the greener grass in there

the supplications fall on dead ears and
ears of dead are but full of clay

why don't you hear when names are
called? and yours comes to the fore,
again

are you afraid, or lazy, or deaf when I
ask for your divine help?

why must I be like in a trance, a
spinning doll, a top made to dance

I ask once more before I am dust:

"Grant me the man whose presence I
lust."

night is too short

the taste of you on my lips still lingers

the longer I wait, the more it grows

the night is too short to make me sated

I fear every night the coming of dawn

///

at risk I turn into a spark

then conflagration lights up the dark

before Aurora lifts her head

my body's cool on ashen bed

the antidote

the side of your bed — warm yet cold

the fire is lacking, the passion — forlorn

how come that you so lonely can be

when antidote is named after me?

///

the winds have risen, the heat is gone

the storm is brewing, the cloaks are off

the dagger shines in Stygian gloom

the watch has changed, poison's
removed

prayers answered

such yearning, one of a kind

prolonged, frustrating, unconscious of
time

I wish to shake off its fetters strong

to part with pain much overlong

///

your presence beckons, I have to go

the prayers answered, now God is gone

and in your arms I made a nest

which keeps me warm, which keeps me
safe

fern flowers

fern flowers on her head, and
surrounded was she by them too

in the depths of forest she reclined,
scents of pines prevailed, awaiting you

were you hiding, lacking courage or did
your shyness conquer you?

in the forest, on the moss bed, she with
you wanted commune

///

little fairies flew around, curious,
twinkling teary eyes

for they knew the wait was over when
they saw the flowers wither

as of bed, the moss grew brittle and by
wind was carried little

to the lands that he now lived in —
message spelling: "Never have been."

litanies, vespers, carols, and praises

prayerfully

he became the practicer of the faith

and she was it

his goddess, his fate

with every turn his worship grew

for he was her slave through and
through

each morning he prayed

each evening too

never enough of hardness of pew

litanies, vespers, carols, and praises

she heard them often, feverish, begging

and granted wishes for holy presence

to him and his prayers, forgetting
penance

naked on your dwelling's step

naked you found me on your dwelling's
step

cold, yet still warm for your hands to
take

in your arms to wrap, to care, and to
stay

I offer myself like moth to a flame

///

at your altar I worshipped for time long
enough

exhausted my strength with waiting
become

but here I am now for you to take

a keepsake, a match, an equal, a stay

when stories were long

there have been times when stories
were long

and ears were accustomed to word
chasing word

there have been times when forests
were virgin

and wildlife throve inside and at its
margin

there have been times when souls were
not yet given

and your and mine danced before they
were riven

now all they do is search and not find

mad, lost, and sad like seashells in sand

the little death

with lifted arms and bated breath

my movements cease, and comes my
death

so little is it that I choose

to welcome it with awe, amused

and when it passes, the flood is over

and what remains is blush all over

I gather strength, I draw on force

to ask to die tonight once more

when petrichor rose

when petrichor rose she danced like
mad

hair streaming wet, dew drops on eyes

no way to tell if she's nymph, hulder,
helloi

if time has stopped, imploded or died

///

what he perceived through thick of trees

were dripping hands and water-stained
lips

drawn was he to her being whole

the ground that drank rain that she stole

///

with silent steps and beating heart

he thus emerged on winded path

at whose conclusion placed was she

dancing naked trippingly

Devil in the flesh

of honey your words seem to me

and even the tears lose their bitter feel

unsour me, make me not-dry

to melt the salt in my veins try

///

drink me like you would champagne at
dawn

full to the brim, roll me on tongue

the hot and cold, the ebb and flow

devour the flesh that Devil's made home

saffron

I am saffron, I am, to your hands and
your eyes

the stigma I bear is all bloody but mine

in your fingers I roll like a thread seeking
eye

for your gaze gives delight and your lips
make me die

the bottom of glass

to the bottom of the glass I, drop

I am heavy, somnolent, drunk from my
fall

with quiet fever I long for your thirst

and to get you drunk I intend from the
first

///

come to me, come to me with fire in
veins

in hurry, in need, in sunshine or rain

come to me, come to me and have a
drop

so from the bottom of glass I could rise
to the top

where courage is scarce

into a phantasy I turn every night

to haunt all your dreams and give you
delight

the hunger I feel is shared and well
known

for we share your bed, yet you are alone

///

in realms of sleep, we meet and we dare

what we don't do here, where courage is
scarce

and so I roam worlds we both occupy

even if it is just for briefness of nights

the beast

in darkness hidden was her shame

then duly swallowed by night's deep well

once it was gone and stayed away

let loose was what she kept at bay

the beast sprang forth, of hungry eyes

of appetite that made the starving blush

and it sought flesh, unbridled, raw

to feast upon with empty maw

when darkness was entirely lifted

she there reclined, naked and listless

awaiting only advent of night

for beast was fed but did not die

la mer d'obscurité

la nuit est pleine de beauté

mon coeur — la mer d'obscurité

pour toi je brûle comme une pensée

qui était cachée dans l'enfer condensé

drink me by the drop

drink me by the drop

thirst is what I wish to stoke

just an ounce and that quite rarely

to allow you to want me madly

///

drop, drop, drop, and then a stop

then I surface to the top

sweet is thirst that then one day

will be quenched by endless rain

frost and void

those nights that we have not yet spent
together

await to happen on earth or in heaven

my side of bed is frosty with cold

and yours is empty, filled with a void

///

to melt, to fill would be the answer

of prayers, wishes to which God's to
pander

in my own corner of frozen world

the heat is raging to burn up your void

the virgin sands of islands lost

the virgin sands of islands lost

whose every grain wants you the most

you tread to reach the waters' depth

to take a dip and dive to its bed

and thus enclosed you writhe and pant

for water's more than you could find

then rise the waves of forces blind

and to the shore you are resigned

we are a territory

we are a territory

made of rock, solitary

just us two, the sun, the moon

circling, tempting

light and gloom

///

no one dares invade our lands

too afraid themselves they find

might they — would encountered such

all their courage promptly crushed

///

for the haven is our own

bed-rock, lava, lust

alone

my armour, shield, and master

the things I choose to leave for myself

one day you may discover

the poems I write and put on the shelf

one day you may uncover

///

for if I let you into my world

I want no reservations

you are to be more than my all

my armour, shield, and master

ma magie

when the words of French rolled off my
tongue

I partook in tasting the sweetest fruit

full of surprises I found the verse

but thought all the time how I'll whisper
in such

for your own ears, pleasures, and
needs:

"J'ai hâte de pouvoir enfin faire ma
magie."

moments pure

in those moments pure, devoid of strife

when life is light and time is stopped

onto love I lean with no end in mind

for the end may be near and increase
my strife

soul between my teeth

with my soul between my teeth

I approach you, I offer a kiss

take it, for it is steaming hot

as if a mist enwrapped us both

///

drink from my well that never ends

drink till your thirst is immensely
quenched

my kingdom visit and stay a while

enthroned I am with you by my side

have you been hunting?

have you been hunting, my dear?

the treasure's awaiting, it's near

for now it is closed and silent

void rules in its depths of darkness

but should a lance appear, fired rightly

it would have been embraced, tightly

and little death would swiftly follow

succeeded by cries of more and more

burnt grass

burnt grass

supporting us but only a little as we float
above

levitation

like lasting ovation, given us by the stars

rozarium

do Jej rozarium zawitał Świt

cichutko zaszeptał, po czym znikł

a chwilę później także Ona

pomiędzy kwiatami w promieniach
słońca

zaczęła się dumnie przechadzać

i nagim ciałem o liście zawadzać

Jej każdy krok wytracał rosę

i rzucał ją pod Jej stopy bose

a kiedy ścieżka dobiegła końca

i poza zasięgiem była już słońca

doleciał do niej na skrzydłach głos:

"Czekałem by dotknąć choć jeden Twój
włos."

po nagim ciele przeszedł Ją dreszcz

wiedziała z czyich ust uciekł ten wiersz

wiedziała także że On tu jest

by Jej róży wręczyć Mu rozkwitły pęk

a shout to sky sweep

if a myriad of stars fell at my feet

and you were the one who gave them to
me

if moon smiled at your foolish deed

for she knew how much of love I have
need

if every night you sowed and you reaped

from out of my lips a shout to sky sweep

I would stay true to nature that's true

in world that comprises of just me and
just you

that Breughel

when you sent that Breughel to my
house

I was surprised to learn you knew what I
liked

and when it was followed by a letter of
love

I knew you knew me better than I
thought

then came the gift I dreamt most of all

you stood in front of the house's door

you took a step toward me and stayed

lost to the world, but gaining new life

islands of shadow

islands of shadow, pools of light

on her body gathered

ready to be traced with manly might

and then covered

///

the night is falling, the blaze is dying

on the bedsheet drenched

the flames that were full of wailing

now lay much quenched

if words could speak

if words could speak

but speak they cannot

they would have said

they'd say a lot

of wanting, of yearning, of soul
destruction

of leaves turning yellow, of hearts'
inaction

///

but there blows wind that spells your
name

embroidered on the winter air

from the beg-inning until the end

of lifespan of the alphabet

///

and when I am in open air

I hear the whispers of your name

and shiver goes down bones that crack

and call your name, from front to back

///

the frost is harsh, the cold is ice

birds' presence is but left to chance

but there's a flicker of warm hope

that you with I could still be roped

in the twilit orchard

in the twilit orchard, barefoot, hot

she trod like a hare when the hunt is on

with silk all over and sun at her feet

between the trees she walked
incomplete

///

when in the silence a low sound came

she knew her nature would be tamed

before he could touch her she turned
around

to whisper: "There's fruit to be had on
the ground."

valley of her spine

in the valley of her spine

droplets gathered, one by one

and he drank them with eyes closed

till his thirst was almost gone

then he turned her naked body

to drink from another valley

land of honey, land of gold

mining for that precious ore

just a verse

you turned me into a verse

with a wave of your hand

and I floated and swayed

on the strength of your breath

I settled gently on page turning white

the darkness of ink into paper thus sank

and I stayed with your forever since

just a verse, by your expression,
evinced

a back arch

her back — an arch but not of marble

a violent rise then slowly descending

you had to hold her hips quite tightly

to stop her short of levitating

honey

sweetness that spread on his tongue

was honey-like, and more

he wanted to have the longer he licked

the quenching of thirst was never
achieved

there came a storm which through
honey rippled

silence ensued then a tiniest of whispers

issued in way akin to begging:

"Now is my turn to take to the drinking."

like knaves

violent spasms that arch her back

up and down, with moans to match

your favourite sight, your dream of
dreams

just yours to behold, like knaves do their
queens

the ribbon

she wore a ribbon around her neck

and then besides nothing else

with shaky fingers he grabbed the
ribbon

and so unpacked the gift him given

inferno

in blazing inferno she awoke

even though world was covered in snow

the fire within ravaged like Huns

who fought better than those with the
guns

plunged was she in tohu-bohu of flames

much too hot to see what was there

when material he became

by the side of infernal blaze

the sweetest of dreams

the sweetest of dreams — the guarded
one

arms close by into which I can fall

eyes that perceive the slumber deep

hands that can catch if I were to slip

///

safety afforded by your solid presence

is like the rock that moves never, never

and so I sleep, enveloped in peace

under the watch that fails to cease

split is the night

in the night you called my name

and I replied, a truthful dare

yet voice so carried through the dream

sounded weak, like bleating sheep

///

why don't you call me with all your
might?

so that with sound split is the night

so that the stars, scared to their bones,

flee and light up some foreign shores

silk trees

among the silk trees you searched for
me

led by the laughter you could well hear

escaping, running I tore my dress

and made you slightly off course digress

but then the trees became quite sparse

and by one's side I stood and glanced

at how you approached with furious
steps

ready to tear what was left of the dress

evil edge

time's evil edge blunted by absence

tears that fall flat on reality's surface

the missing is felt as pain's sharpest
shoot

with stars unaiding to find the right route

whisper in the night

in the fullness of the night

came a voice akin to cry

of desire grand it spoke

begging, moving

word by word

///

then word right through darkness came

tender whisper of my name

and to you I flew like shot

of more words need there was not

Lethe

having drunk from Lethe, come to me

rest your head on my bosom and tired
sleep

may you dream of adventures yet
unconceived

of the lands you will visit alone or with
me

Stymphalian birds

Stymphalian birds - cruel, strong

with metal wings and beaks of bronze

at service mine are when I want

to capture you and make my own

black lace

black lace, so much in contrast

with body resting against the white but

when it's gone and whiteness is us

blackness dances in the sky

autumn fruit

"Je préfère tes fruits, Automne,
Aux fleurs banales du Printemps!"* he
said

and my heart was more than fed

with words that gave thoughts their
bread

because you know that there's nothing
wrong

with growing old

///

I too like autumn, more than any other
season

when the nature heaves with the fruit of
reason

*After Baudelaire's "Le Monstre, ou le
Paranymphe d'une nymphe macabre".

...

asleep

yet awaken by your kiss

that silently settled

on the side of my neck

a feeble strap

a strap so feeble that down it goes

down shoulder pale yet hot like coals

are you afraid of catching fire?

no, you are not — your lips I require

rhyme chasing rhyme

imagine a little cottage, us two

a forest, a garden, and meadow in
bloom

imagine a walk, a stroll, and a kiss

that has for a witness the lake and the
trees

imagine a room, just for us two

a table, two chairs, and bed undisturbed

imagine a gaze, a gesture, and whisper

that calls you toward me with spell full of
fever

///

imagine then waking by my naked side

in world that consists of rhyme chasing
rhyme

the key

hours have passed since I saw you last

but hunger I feel is not a thing of the past

it gnaws and it bores, it turns me to dust

for you know that hours have already passed

///

the evening is ripe and growing old

the shadows are long and growing strong

the hour has come when you come to me

and time departs leaving the key

my sky

skycold eyes, in opposition

yet they are to me my sky

rays that run away but stay there

harbingers of happy time

if I ruled you

if I ruled you, you would prosper

like a land of gold and water

you would find that peace that wars hate

marred with laughter, growing stronger

///

if I ruled you, you would triumph

like a warrior who slays the king

you would find what you desire:

happiness that only love brings

Circe

prowl

around

and in and out

so docile, and the world astound

my house is built of Carrara's gift

to withstand the passage of time

murmurations

"If not, winter…,"* she whispered

and the snow began to fall

heavy like the coal that listens

to the steps of light that's cold

///

"If not, winter…," she murmured

and the starlings took their flights

light as coin tossed down a deep well

settling gently, missing rime

*After Sappho.

my witchery is now complete, of your
hand I let go and disappear, may you
remain under my spell and words that I
uttered haunt your days

A.

www.ingramcontent.com/pod-product-compliance
Lightning Source LLC
LaVergne TN
LVHW021515080426
835509LV00018B/2518